Get Up & Get After It

Discover and Thrive with a DRIVEN mindset

By Ryan Ricks

TABLE OF CONTENTS

DEDICATION 1

ACKNOWLEDGEMENTS 2

INTRODUCTION 3

DEVELOPING A DRIVEN MINDSET 10

DESIRE 16

READY TO CHANGE 22

INTENTIONAL THOUGHTS 27

VISUALIZATION 32

EXCITED TO EXECUTE 36

    EXCITED 37

    EXECUTION 39

NO EXCUSES, NEVER QUIT 42

ABOUT THE AUTHOR 47

DEDICATION

Dedicate the Book to my Dad, Clarence Ricks JR.
My First role model.

ACKNOWLEDGEMENTS

I would like to acknowledge God. Without God I would be nothing, who gave me this vision to write this book in my sleep. My wife, Leticia Ricks who is the love of my life and is an inspiration to me. My Kids Leila, Rya and Princeton. I love yall with all my heart. Also, my mom, Barbara Ricks, for her never-ending support and love. Thank you, Mom. I love you.

INTRODUCTION

The life we live is precious. It is something we should never take for granted. Aren't you breathing? Are you not able to see and touch the words on this page? Did you not have the ability to turn to this page in the first place? These thoughtless things are constantly underappreciated by all of us. Well, not everyone has these luxuries. Someone may not have that capability or may have lost that ability today. And unfortunately, they will not gain that back. Be thankful for God's grace and your ability to do so much now. Indeed, God has more for you, and you should want more for yourself.

> "Our God is able to do exceedingly abundantly above all we ask or think" — Ephesians 3:20

Every morning at 5 am, I aim to encourage everyone to "get up and get after it". This is solely due to the impact motivation and movement have made on my life. Being gracious and having gratitude for the ability to simply get out of bed in the morning will forever be present in my thoughts. It hits home differently for me because I was physically incapable of doing so at one point in my life. Through this book, I will reveal my secret to constantly winning that mental battle every day that keeps me motivated, disciplined, and excited to execute my biggest dreams into a reality. You can have it too.

As a young kid born in the mid-80s, I was extremely active—most of the 80s babies were. We would choose to be outdoors with friends over indoors with T.V. and video games daily. Disciplining kids was simple back then. Restricting us to the house was the worst our parents and guardians could do. However, these days, it's the complete opposite case. An active lifestyle was my birthright, and my dad, a passionate physical education teacher, dictated the only option in my house. Be sure never to mistakenly call him simply a "gym teacher." He would quickly clarify for you, "I don't teach a gym." I educate students on the proper movements of the human body through physical activity." He earned and demanded respect from parents and students alike. I can vividly recall doing pull-ups on my dad's arm from the age of 2 or 3. Watching him do push-ups of 100 at a time. Waking up every Saturday morning before 6 am to get a head start on the day. He would always say, "The early bird gets the worm." Indeed, your environment plays a massive role in what is considered normal as a young child.

I participated in as many sports as possible: martial arts, soccer, basketball, baseball, you name it; I did it in some capacity. While playing, I was in my natural element. Everything came easy to me, and so everything was fun. My parents would sign me up for almost anything, especially if it was free.

It was the fall of 1994, and I was just 9 years old. Soccer season had just begun, and I was picked to play on the travel team. It was the season's first game, and I still remember it as if it were yesterday. There must have been a monsoon that day. I remember it due to the torrential rain and wind throughout the duration of the game. This was before they canceled games due to the weather conditions and slippery fields. I played the whole game, and we won. Later that night, I woke up with a deep, constant, unbearable pain in my left foot. I got out of bed to seek out my mother, and as I began to walk, I was limping with tons of discomfort. It was extremely agonizing. My mother, who worked for an orthopedic doctor, didn't hesitate and brought me to him the next morning. There was a noticeable shift to my big toe, curling inward toward my second toe and swelling around my ankle. They did X-rays, and the doctor saw nothing structurally wrong. He thought it was just a sprain from playing and sent us home to wait it out.

Weeks passed, and there was no improvement. The excruciating pain would return randomly, so pain relief medications were introduced to me very early in life. They ran test after test, trying to figure out what was behind the extreme discomfort. After multiple opinions, tests, X-rays, MRIs, and blood panels, the doctor suggested seeing a rheumatologist. At the time,

I had no idea what that even was. There, we finally received a prognosis of what I had been dealing with the whole time. I was diagnosed with juvenile rheumatoid arthritis (JRA) about one month after the initial night of pain. It was a pretty rare condition in the mid-90s.

Apparently, this was a part of my genetic makeup, and the combination of rain, dampness, and activity just woke it up. JRA, which my dad would soon nickname "Arthur," is an autoimmune disease that tricks your body into thinking that something bad is happening internally and makes your immune system mistakenly attack your joints. If left untreated, it could cause permanent joint damage. At 9 years old, I was totally naive but anxiously asked, "How do we fix it so I can get back to playing sports?" The doctor took me out of all physical activity. I couldn't even participate in P.E. or recess activities. I was utterly crushed and 100% cut off from what I loved to do: playing sports and going outside with my friends. I was extremely sad and discouraged beyond belief. At the time, I still couldn't grasp the severity of the situation, mainly because there would be times I felt that I could play. It wasn't until a few months later that Arthur's symptoms came into full force. I can clearly recall times when I was in so much pain and discomfort that I could not get out of bed. Even turning over in bed was excruciatingly painful. I can still feel tears drop from the pain as I remember trying to walk to the bathroom. My dad often picked me up to take me into a bathtub to get an Epsom salt bath to help relieve the discomfort. In high school, severe flare-ups forced me to go to school with crutches or canes just to get from class to class. Classmates asked what happened and why I had no cast. Everyone followed up with the same comment when I told them I had an arthritis flare-up. Isn't arthritis for old people? "Clearly not," I would sarcastically respond. Some flare-ups lasted for a week, and some lasted a few days. It was never consistent timing but was always consistently unpleasant.

After many years of prayer, healthy nutrition choices, an active lifestyle, and the will to live a quality lifestyle, my rheumatologist, Dr. Sullivan of Edison, NJ, deemed me in remission at age 15. This meant I didn't have to take medication unless it was absolutely needed. This was huge because the prior medicine prescribed affected my growth as an adolescent. I remember the best advice given to me was by Dr. Sullivan when she told me, "The more active you stay, the better off you will be as you age." Those words are implanted in my brain. Applying those words has made the most impact on my life. Today, I have an abundance of days with no pain or discomfort due to my healthy lifestyle. Flare-ups now only arise once or twice a year, lasting only a day or two. The grace of God and my active, healthy lifestyle have made my life phenomenal.

My overall appreciation for being able to "get up and get after it" every morning motivates me and keeps me disciplined. On pain-free days when I feel lazy, I lean on those tough, painful days as a kid to serve as a constant reminder that I was once unable to stand up. Every day, I choose not to take it for granted, and neither should you. It is my purpose to encourage others to do the same. My mission is to serve everyone by unlocking their potential to grow daily and achieve their desired success. It can be life-transforming to simply wake up with a purpose and plan to get a little bit better each and every day. Remember to never take your everyday habits for granted. I appreciate this ultimate blessing and am grateful to have the ability to actually get up and get after it—the "I.T." being LIFE ITSELF.

Now, looking back almost 30 years, I naturally adopted a DRIVEN mindset. I chose not to be a JRA victim and intentionally reminded myself I would be victorious in this fight. The daily reminder to be DRIVEN kept me persistent, accountable, and passionate about achieving my goals and living my life to the fullest. First, I had a desire to get back to playing sports pain-free. Secondly, readiness. I was ready to make the change I had control of, and accept my current circumstance. I was ready to change my diet and amount of activity and implement new forms of activity, such as swimming. Next, I had to have an intentional state of mind. Arthur was not going to affect me my whole life. My mind was made up. I would be better; I would beat JRA. No. Matter. What.

My visions of Michael Jordan and Emmitt Smith posters on my wall reminded me that consistency and persistence were the keys to always winning. When I had no symptoms, I was constantly excited to execute any time I was able to do sports. No excuses were allowed to take up real estate in my brain. To quit was never an option, thanks to my dad. And therefore, I dedicate this book to him.

DEVELOPING A DRIVEN MINDSET

Developing a DRIVEN mindset is a conscious weapon that you need to adopt and leverage. This will make a transformational impact on your life. Throughout the professional years of my life in the health and fitness business, which I like to refer to as the business of people, I have come to realize that it's less about what people do and more about the impactful thoughts they carry around that drives them to reach and exceed their goals. Being fortunate to have trained and coached a wide demographic of individuals through my 18-year career has allowed me to analyze the driving force behind their decision to partake in and maintain a healthy lifestyle. Whether young, old, athletes, disabled, corporate professionals, blue-collar workers, or diseased people, the most successful ones always have the same thing driving them. Their mindset is in the right place at the right time. Regardless of whether it is conscious or subconscious, they are triggered by a thought, a mindset that allows them to adapt and accept health and fitness habits. Their thoughts create a driving force that will dramatically influence their decisions about how to live their lives in the present and the future. Multiple factors come together to cause an inspired self-intervention.

For instance, I trained a man named Aaron. Before training with me, he had never stepped inside a health facility. His prior activity was limited only to a casual walk around the neighborhood. One day, he went to the doctor for an annual check-up. He discovered his blood pressure was dangerously high, and he had been diagnosed with type 2 diabetes. This led the doctor to prescribe him medications that would control both. But Aaron, who hated the idea of taking medicine, decided to take the holistic approach by starting a healthy lifestyle. He started by eating nutritious foods and exercising daily. After that, everything changed. Aaron became a gym fanatic, working out daily on his own and training with mentors. He was committed to living naturally and not taking medicine for the rest of his life. He also had a dream to walk his daughter down the aisle when she was ready to get married. She was only a freshman in high school at the time, but his mindset did not waiver, not even a little bit. His vision was crystal clear. After a year of consistency, Aaron lost over 70 lbs. He decreased his blood pressure, and his blood sugar levels also began to stabilize without any medications. The DRIVEN mindset kept him from quitting and falling back into his old habits that would have led him back to the road of illness.

Everyone's story is always different, but what they share is that they wake up one morning and tell themselves that enough is enough; the change starts today. Their mind is made up and they will do whatever it takes to change their ways. They choose consistent sacrifices over simple satisfaction. They gain the drive to be comfortable with being uncomfortable. They know it will not be easy, and there may be a struggle, but they decide to strategize for success. They lose ambivalence and gain the determination that a person can only acquire and maintain within themselves. An outside factor or extrinsic motivator may start the journey, but then intrinsic motivation takes over, and this maintains the life-changing habit. The motivation to stay consistent must come from within.

I've always said you can never force someone to do something they don't want to do. For a deliberate action to persist and accelerate, it must come from within. Too often, we live in a stagnant, mundane place of comfort. When you get into your car, turn it on, and put it into drive, very little happens without hitting the accelerator. We then press the gas pedal until we obtain a certain speed before easing up, so we can comfortably cruise. Many times during our life, we start our engine and get into the driving seat, but our normal habits and routines keep us idling. We forget to keep our foot on the pedal to accelerate ourselves to excellence. We then only use enough of our energy to fulfill those simple actions. But later, as we go down the road in life, we might want to achieve a higher level of success in our personal or professional lives. Indeed, life is a complicated landscape, not a smooth path, full of waves and downslopes. With a DRIVEN mindset, you can consciously accelerate your personal will. That will is going to lead you to a constant upward trajectory in your life, with a never-ending pursuit of all your desires and a steady self-account-ability focus.

During my 18 years working as a personal trainer, God has shown me this vision of mastering a DRIVEN mindset for success in achieving goals. The DRIVEN mindset is the daily foundational consciousness that prepares you mentally, physically, and spiritually. It gives you the ability to intentionally remind yourself of the importance and urgency with which your goals and desires must be met. It helps you to be all in and stop at nothing until your goals are achieved. When life throws you off course (which is completely normal) or when you begin to doubt your capabilities, honing in on your DRIVEN mindset resets your consciousness and keeps you on track for success.

The *D* in DRIVEN stands for Desire. Actualizing what your dreams and desires are in the beginning is essential. Being truthful and open allows them to be as big as possible. The *R* in DRIVEN is for Readiness. This can be a tough question for all of us. Are we actually ready to change? Are we ready to make the sacrifices that come along? Are we ready for everything that comes our way in order to be successful? The letter *I* stands for the ability to be Intentional. Internally and externally. The power of our intentional thoughts and actions needs to be channeled through our every move. The *V* in DRIVEN helps with Visualization. Simply put, seeing is believing and without vision, you will have no clear direction to reach success. Now, *E* in the word is E-squared. It stands for Excited to Execute. The enthusiastic mindset while executing everything makes us fall in love with our process. Lastly, the N in DRIVEN reminds us to make No excuses and to Never quit.

Each letter has relevance and power of its own. Combined and applied, they are life-transforming. Each supports the other on your ability to mentally master your journey. You will set out and achieve all of your goals. I'm sure you have heard the saying, "You can do it if you put your mind to it." Mastering your mindset is essential to your long-term and sustainable success. Your mind is one of the strongest weapons you have at your disposal. We have the power to talk ourselves into or out of something. We have Godly thoughts and not-so-Godly thoughts. The mind forms thoughts and ideas that can manipulate you to do things you may not normally do. It can make you go from rational to irrational in an instant. Harnessing the power of staying DRIVEN in your mindset will help you reach your goals. Your positivity and passion for life will also radiate off you and affect others. Loved ones, co-workers, and friends will see and feel the contagious shift of your positive energy on display. Like a chain, this can help transfer your positive impact, excellence and energy to others.

As I lay out the basics of having a DRIVEN mindset, I want you to think deeply about exactly what you want to achieve in your life. Think and dream big in all aspects of your life. What do you want for your health and fitness goals? What do you want, financially and professionally? Where do you want to be, spiritually and personally? Whatever it is, think about what it means for you. Focus on building your DRIVEN mindset daily, and you will reap all the benefits. Now let's get up, and get after it!

DESIRE

The first piece in our puzzle of success is the desire for it. We have strong feelings of wanting something in our lives. What do you want the most in your life? What do you want to accomplish? What would you like to change in your current situation? In Napoleon Hills' masterpiece *Think and Grow Rich*, he studied the richest and most successful people of his time. The main factor that was common in all of them was their burning desire to achieve their goals and set themselves apart. Your desires are conscious thoughts as well as subconscious thoughts. We realize what we want is our consciousness. Our subconscious thoughts can easily sway our actions, preventing us from executing our true desires.

An easy example is sitting comfortably on the couch late at night, and our conscious mind kicks in and says, "I want something to eat." Then our subconscious will combat it, "But I'm so comfortable and don't want to get up." Has this ever happened to you? Therefore, you end up waiting until you need to eat something, or you wait to call someone else to get you something to eat. Even though the goal of getting something to eat will be met, the personal alignment of your conscious and subconscious mind is off balance. Our desires need to be clearly identified. Is there a greater purpose for your desire? Are you truly passionate about the desire you are looking to achieve? How much can this desire shape and change your life and the lives of those around you? All great questions must be answered and precisely written down before you embark on your journey to achieve your desires.

These answered questions will be the daily motivation that will allow you to train your subconscious to align with your consciousness on the importance and sense of urgency needed to reach your desires. Then, ask yourself why it's important to you. Once you have your initial *why*, dive in deeper. Ask yourself why again. Peel back that onion to find that deep underlying reason. For example, somebody might say, "I want to be healthy." "Why do you want to be healthy?" "I want to be healthy so I can move around and not have pain." "Why do you want to move around and not have pain?" "I want to move around without pain so that I can feel better." "Why is it important for you to feel better?" "It is important for me to feel better so I don't feel tired and sluggish when my kids run all over the place." "Why is that important to you?" "I want to be the father who plays with his kids into his fifties." "Why is it important for you to play with them into your fifties?" The questions will get more important as you go on. Every next question will ignite a deeper fire and give you the strength to pursue your desires.

"It's important for me to play with them in my fifties because my parents always complained of back pain when I was young. They could never actively play with me outside." There it is; that is the answer right there!" The deep desire that you want to be around for your kids to play with because you want for them something better than what you had. Finding that deep-rooted underlying purpose of our desires is what we will need to push and motivate us. We must keep these thoughts in our brains to achieve our desired goals. When you have the will, you will find a way. God will also bless you and find a way out of no way. More often than not, we have desires that are not strong enough. They are not big enough or don't mean enough to us to really achieve them. Most of us desire to be better than we are now. New desires are revealed to us when we are backed into a corner and have no way out of there. There was a time when I had no heat in my apartment throughout the winter season. It was a situation that I would never allow myself to be in again.

The desire is to always be comfortable in the home and warm in the winter. We also change when we have a challenge that we need to face head-on. It may be a tragic car accident that affects our cognitive motor skills. Your desire then would be to improve the motor skills you had before that accident. The challenge could also be a financial pitfall that leads you to almost bankruptcy, forcing you to find other ways to earn more income and not spend as much. Our desires must stay within us and motivate us to push through and do better for ourselves. When your family is relying on you financially, the desire to take care of them and fulfill their needs will drive you and motivate you to achieve greatness for them. How badly do you actually want it? I want us to think about a child and how they always desire things. Have you ever seen or been in a shopping store with a child? Every toy they see, they just want it, no? They see it, and now that it is in their grasp, they believe it should be theirs. They don't understand it has to be paid for; they just know right there at that very moment, and they want it.

Typically, a child's imagination and desires are so strong that nothing is outside their reach. They may even go to the length of throwing themselves on the floor or a temper tantrum. They will go to any lengths to get what they desire, even if it is embarrassing you in public. That is exactly what we need to do as adults. I'm not saying you should throw yourself on the floor. But we need to start having that imagination and believing that nothing is outside our reach. Our goals should be so big that they trigger fear and doubt, making us say, "That will be hard." It should be, and it will be. If it doesn't challenge you, it will not change you. Nothing is outside of our reach. Just reach out in hopes of accomplishing your goals. You need to make leaps toward what you want to achieve. Hone in on those deep desires. If your "Why?" is not strong enough, your purpose for achieving that desire is not strong enough. Once you are honest with yourself and reveal those deep underlying feelings of importance to achieve that goal, do not lose sight of it. It should remain forever present in your consciousness. These are the desires we must prioritize.

We will have other desires that will not have the same meaning, so they will be easier for us to give up on or set aside for a later time. From my experience, people often set out and achieve a goal because it's the popular thing to do. Everyone is always talking about it. "I want to lose weight," "I want to have financial freedom," "I want to be wealthy." They go with all the popular buzzwords. What direct connection and purpose do you have with such desires? Why are these desires important to you? What will your relentless motivation be when you have your first obstacle to continue on the path to reach your set desire? In human nature, having the desire is the easy part. Being relentless in fulfilling it is a rare quality found only in people who are truly driven. People say they always want to lose weight but won't change their eating habits or workout daily. Most people want financial freedom but aren't willing to explore opportunities to make more money, which means they are fine working paycheck to paycheck. These are prime examples that your deep underlying importance of the desires is not strong enough. That feeling for your desires needs to be so painfully strong that it hurts you if you don't achieve it. Ask yourself, "Are my desires strong enough that I'm willing to take a leap, step out, have faith, and achieve the goal that scares me the most?" Be willing to be challenged. Be willing to change for the better. Do I have that drive within me to reach all my desires?

I can do all things through Christ who strengthens me. Philippians 4:13.

Action Items. Ask yourself these questions and write them down on paper. What are your desires? What do you want to achieve? Circle top 3. Then ask yourself *why* 5 times for each one. Once you have peeled back the onion to the core, turn your *why* into one big sentence. Make your sentence visibly present daily. Set alarms on your phone with the sentence to appear hourly. Make your desires your primary focus.

READY TO CHANGE

Are you ready to change? Let's be honest: are you really ready to utilize everything you have, every opportunity, every resource you have, and use it to your full advantage? Are you willing to give up things you are accustomed to doing that are getting in your way of success? Are you willing to shut some people out that get in your way from being successful? Are you really ready to achieve what you truly desire? When you look up the word *ready* in the dictionary, you will find words like '*action*' and '*prepared*.' When you look up the word *change* in the dictionary, you will come across phrases like 'to do *something different*' and 'be *something different*.' Most take action daily. Preparing for strategic-specific action is, however, usually forgotten.

Most of the time, we do what is pleasing in the present time, at the sacrifice of what we want to achieve for our future. We let them get in the way of what we want. That's what we call instant gratification. We want the momentary reward. It's just that it is only for a moment. The more we hold off on what we want for the moment, we will really see our true desires come to fruition. Our readiness-to-change mentality must convert to prepared actions. They cannot be thoughtless actions. They must be organized and planned. They need to be reflective of the lifestyle we want to live. We must ask ourselves, what is getting in our way of achieving our desires? What barriers might I face? What situations will come up that will possibly distract my focus? Who would not be the most supportive of my growth and goals? You should ask yourself these crucial questions to unveil your path to success. If we truly want to reach what we set out to do, we have to think, move, and act differently.

How do we do this? We must be decisive, disciplined, and committed to our goals and desires. Relentless even. Forming new habits that align with the person we wish to become. If you want something you have never had, you must be willing to do things you have never done before.

For example, Do you want to be healthier? Ask yourself what healthy people do. What do healthy people eat? What are the lifestyle choices that healthier people live by? What disciplines do they stick to that allow them to maintain their way of life? Habits! Interviewing a healthy person or researching healthy people should answer these questions for you. Once those questions are answered, write down everything you currently do in your life that does not align with your goal. Remember to be brutally honest with yourself. If you are not honest with yourself, your purpose for achieving your goal is not strong enough. As such, you are not ready to change.

Once you have your list of traits that need work, you might have one thing, or it may be twenty. Select one to two things that will be the easiest to accomplish. Focus each day to fulfill that change to begin the process. You must consciously prepare and evaluate what and who may distract you from accomplishing your new task. Identify who will be supportive. The more supportive people you have around you, the better. We want positive influences in our journey that will help us understand the importance and purpose of self-growth. Your best supporters will actually hold you accountable, even if their words seem harsh to you. The more people you tell about your new habits, the more likely you are to stick with the habit because you are becoming more mentally bought in. Others will not be supportive; that is usually because they like you the way you were when you didn't have the desire to change. The hardest part for them is the new habit you are taking on will affect how you may relate to each other. Going out to eat at restaurants or happy hours after work instead of going to the gym. You are spending more time developing yourself than spending time with them. As you are honest with yourself, honesty with them is important as well. Communicating (common action) your *why* behind the change will be crucial for your relationship. People can't understand what they don't know. So do not just shut them out; let them in 100%. You can actually inspire them and now have an affiliate and an accountability partner. The trans theoretical model of change. It revolves around pre-contemplation, contemplation, preparation, action, and maintenance stages.

In the pre-contemplation stage, the person is not even thinking of making a change. It is not even a conscious thought in their mind that they need to change. In the contemplation phase, people start thinking they might need to change. They are starting to consciously think it might be a good idea to change their life around, and they start wanting that change. We prepare, look up, and research things in the preparation stage to start a new behavior. In the action stage, we do just that: we take planned actions to fulfill our desires and look for opportunities to maintain these activities. Lastly, in the maintenance stage, when they are pretty much in power to do it on their own, they keep their habits and stay consistent.

Are you Ready to educate? Education is always a vital part of our growth process. Without education, there is only stagnation.

Are you Ready to commit? Another aspect of readiness to change is the readiness to commit. Commitment takes discipline.

Are you Ready for success? With every success comes more respon-sibility. We have to be prepared once we hit the success we desire.

What stage are you at?

Action items:

Ask yourself, what must I do to get to the action stage? What barriers in my life are preventing me from achieving my desires? What has to happen to remove these barriers? What positive things am I going to replace these barriers with? What is consuming my 24 hours? What have I done today to get better? What should I be doing? What am I going to do? Say it 50 times, every day and every night.

INTENTIONAL THOUGHTS

Intentional thoughts lead to intentional actions. My dad always used the term, "Think before you speak." This would stop my siblings or me from being too fast to talk. It would eventually save us from getting in trouble. It mainly would be, "Before you say something stupid, slow down, think twice, and correct yourself." We had to be intentional before opening our mouths to yield the best response possible to save ourselves from reaping any backlash from him.

Definition of intentional: *deliberate, calculated, conscious, done on purpose, planned, studied, purposeful and premeditated.*

Once we know our desires and are truly ready to change, we need to reprogram our thoughts to be positive and calculated to the desires we seek. Our thoughts and words coming into our conscious mind can be used to excel in our lives and achieve our goals faster and further.

Positive thoughts are what we need to keep our hope and faith. We lean on hope and faith to get us through our toughest times. I have always believed in God since I was young. It must have been the Christian school I attended at the age of four that built the foundation, and it stuck. I had faith that God was with me; he knew and saw everything. My parents would remind me, "Lie if you want, but God hears and sees everything." We were not churchgoers. We never found a church home, as my mom would say. My walk with Christ didn't grow stronger until I was close to my 30s. I have my wife to thank for that. She grew up in a very faith-based family that frequently attended church, and not just on Sundays. Most people use Sunday service to get that good word. It resets our intentions and redirects us to focus on God and be thankful for what we have. Keep your faith in Him, for God has a plan for all our lives, and he will be you through the upcoming week. We could all use that positive message to take with us into the coming week. The pastor says, "God answers prayers and will not leave or forsake you." It is generally faith-based motivational speaking one day a week. We can speak motivation, positivity, faith, and hope into ourselves daily. Every moment can be an opportunity. The more we think in positive affirmations, such as "I will be successful," "I will achieve my goals," "I am the best," "I am a winner," and "I never quit," the more our mind stays steadfast on them.

Are you someone who procrastinates every day, constantly putting things off? I would start by saying, "Do it now," every morning, every night, 50 times for 30 days. See if you begin to avoid procrastinating as much. If you spend too much time mindlessly scrolling through your phone, say, "Put it down" 50 times every morning and 50 times every night. Do you have a doubt when you try to get something done? Say, "I got this." Do you have worry or fear hit your mind? Say, "Fear does not exist here." The more we put these intentional thoughts and words in our minds, the more we will believe and be able to move that needle forward toward success. We will conquer procrastination, mindlessness, laziness, doubt, and fear.

Intentionally speaking life into ourselves will help us stay positive and focused. Using strong and empowering words on a day-to-day basis literally changes our mood. If someone asks, "How are you?" we should never say good or okay. There should be no more good and okay. If we are driven to be the best we can be, we should 100% be better than good or okay. We need to be great. We need to be awesome, amazing, phenomenal, excellent, and exceptional. It hits so differently, not just for your mindset but also for the person asking. The energy shift of positivity takes over the area. Intentional thinking before speaking will allow us to shift the energy and the environment around us. I love the quote: "Your attitude will determine your altitude." It means going into everything with a bad attitude is likely going to result in a bad outcome. With a positive attitude, you will begin to be limitless. The power of positive thinking is huge. Keeping a positive attitude is not always the easiest thing. There are going to be times of negativity that come into your mindset. The most important part is to recognize the negativity. If we recognize it, we can begin to fight against negative thoughts.

Being grateful for being able to do things not all people can do can shift your feelings. We are blessed to do so much. Be thankful and appreciative. Show it. Be intentional. We must turn negative thoughts into positive pursuits to achieve our goals and desires. There will always be pain at some point in our lives. We must turn pain into passion. Our feelings get hurt all the time. Turn that hurt into hunger. The more struggles we go through, the more opportunity we have to build strategies to get through the struggles. We will constantly face trials daily, but you will come out triumphant. We will not be a victim anymore; we will be victorious. Remember that anyone successful has probably been through tough times as well. They learned to manage their emotions, turn all negative times into learning experiences, and become positive assets in their lives.

Hold on to the pain, hurt, struggle, and challenges as a constant reminder of why your desire must be achieved. Doing this lets you control your destiny, future, and emotions. The negative thoughts will no longer hold us down; we will use them to accelerate our relentless pursuit to achieve our desires.

Our intentional thought process is key to creating daily habits that align with our dreams and goals.

Positive affirmations must be repeated in our heads and out of our mouths throughout the day. I highly encourage you to be intentional with the words you speak. Do not think small; think big. "I am the best corporate executive." "I am a seven-figure earner." "I am dedicated to growing daily and influencing everyone around me." Intentional thoughts are the start of making intentional actions toward our desires.

VISUALIZATION

Visualize the future you want for yourself. The definition of visualizing is to form a mental image of what you desire. When we have our desire and our mind is prepared thoroughly by getting ready with all aspects, and we have been speaking intentionally to do so, visualization to achieving our goals should be the next step in your journey to be truly driven. It is not easy to visualize your future. However, 65% of the general population are visual learners. This means that seeing information and possessions helps to attain them. Imagine you lived on a block where everyone owned a mansion and a Rolls-Royce. Seeing this daily makes it a normalized goal for you. There would be no doubt that the mansion and the Rolls-Royce are well within your reach. Hence, you clearly have to see your desires coming to fruition. Visualize yourself three months from now, one year from now, five years from now, and twenty years from now to be able to work to attain it. If we don't see it, we won't achieve it. Believe it, see it, and then go out and achieve it. Are we simply passing the time or optimizing your time? There are multiple ways to influence yourself and keep a disciplined mindset through visual reminders and motivators. They will help you see them daily and keep you striving toward your desires.

A great place to start is by thinking about what it would feel like once your desires are fulfilled and your goals are achieved. What emotions would you feel once you have reached your goal? What would your life be like? How would your life be different? Think about a year from now. How would you feel about yourself? These answers will be the appeal we need to excite us and push us to acquire our desires.

Daily visual reminders are helpful to keep your vision alive. Have your smart goals written down so you can see them daily, preferably morning and night. Build a vision board with pictures and words that represent your desired future. A visual checklist for small goals reached with rewards attached to them for completion every month. Break down a year's goal in examples of a breakdown to get there.

Visuals that surround you daily will motivate you to stay on task. Remind yourself to have a sense of urgency each and every day. A checklist will continue to give you direction on what needs to be done to stay connected to your end goal. Another visual that helps keep us positive throughout our journey is positive, powerful words of affirmation. Words like 'strong,' 'relentless,' 'determined,' and 'consistent' have a sense of power. These words should be visible to us every day. Post-it notes work great on the dashboard of your car. Positive mantras are words we can live by to keep us on our mission. We need to see them visibly.

There are many visualizations that can steer us off our path and distract us. These distractions need to be limited. Television, social media, and food ads can stir us in the wrong direction. Television is for entertainment purposes. It drags us in, and we begin to spiral down into overconsumption. The more we consume, the less time we have to work on our true desires and dreams. We need social media to help us achieve our goals if it involves our business. But it is very easy to fall into the wormhole of scrolling. Being mindful of mindless consumption is vital to staying persistent in our pursuit of a better life. If we are on a journey to clear up our eating habits by staying away from fast food restaurants, we don't need to stay away from social media ads that have food in them. Healthy foods and snacks in our car and multiple places around the house will remind us to stay on track. Again, seeing is believing. Like the camera lens, focusing on a visual image lets us see our picture clearly. Our brain and our eyes need to see that vision clearly in order for us to stay focused on the desires we want to achieve. There are settings on the camera that blur out everything around that one focal point. Adjustments need to be made to a camera to help the photographer bring the ultimate vision to life. That is what we need to do for our environment. Make constant adjustments that will block out all the blurriness around us to keep our focus on our goals and desires. Adding all of these visual aids around us makes that constant focus more prevalent than ever before. We begin to move differently and act differently. That vision will get so clear and so profound that we begin to get anxious and overjoyed for what is to come in the future. It is that last reminder before we clearly act on our desires and dreams. We are now excited to execute.

EXCITED TO EXECUTE

Now, the fun begins. All the preparation work you have done to this point has not been easy and has taken some time. You've done great so far, and the hard work is almost over. I'm not a fan of the saying, but this is where the magic needs to happen—that execution phase. We must deliver.

EXCITED

A feeling of great enthusiasm and eagerness. It is always easier to do something when we are excited about our execution. We must love the process. We should know our dreams and desires if we have gone through the earlier chapters. That should be our motivation. We put the effort in to be ready and prepared for whatever needs to be done in order to start working toward our dreams and desires. That's taken care of. We are already being intentional with our thoughts and speaking life and positivity into ourselves that nothing will stop us. We should constantly have a clear visual focus on what we want from our lives; to evolve through thought and external aids. If these steps don't excite you about executing, start again from the D in DRIVEN. Keep going through those steps until you believe it and want it so bad that the excitement is unbearable.

I think back to when I was a young boy around Christmas. I had the desire and dream to get a new bike. I was so ready for Christmas morning. I did all the chores to lay the groundwork leading up to it. I made sure that my grades were on point. I waited hand and foot for my parents to say that I was the best a boy could be. I had no doubt in my mind that the bike would be under the tree. I intentionally talked about that bike to my parents nonstop throughout the last month. I visibly left the magazine open to the page with the bike on it right on top of the kitchen table. How excited do you think I was the night before Christmas? This is the level of excitement that you must have. You must have no doubt in your mind that you were getting that bike. We need that no-doubt mentality in our thoughts day in and day out that our dreams will come to fruition. With that excited mindset, the execution will follow. Every morning, we need to get up and get after it with excitement for the work we need to accomplish. This is what will lead us to our ultimate goals; the small things done consistently will turn into big-time results.

EXECUTION

To carry out fully and put completely into effect a plan.

Execution can often be a daunting task. Some tasks are complex and involve planning and education. Some tasks take more expertise, while some seem impossible. All things are possible with God, faith, and a DRIVEN mindset. Executing at a high and constant level takes a massive amount of discipline. Discipline cannot be broken. It should not allow you to procrastinate. The word "Discipline" comes from "*Discipulus*," the Latin word for pupil, which also provided the source of the word disciple (albeit by way of a late Latin sense-shift to "a follower of Jesus Christ in his lifetime"). In the ancient Hebrew of Proverbs, discipline means instructing, correcting, chastising, or rebuking. It does not mean punishing or beating. In the execution stage, we must exercise all our resources to achieve our goals. We must continue to educate, be relentless, and ask for help from others. We must have a team around us that will challenge, motivate, and hold us accountable to our goals, desires, and dreams. And you must do the same for them. I am blessed for my wife; she is this to me, and I am that to her. I will not let her quit to have a multimillion-dollar travel retreat company just as she stayed with me to write this book. With accountability partners, execution will not waiver. They want to see you succeed as badly as you want to succeed. Execute not just for you.

When in the execution stage, you will need to look back to your deepest *why* questions almost every day for the burning desire of why you are going so hard. The constant reminder is non-negotiable. When we slightly forget the deepest why, what we are trying to achieve feels urgent. You need a sense of urgency. There is no later. There is no tomorrow. There is no next week. I can only *do it now*. We will have doubts and failures. We must start back from the D in Desire and work our way all the way back to the excitement before the execution. You will always get up and get after when done repeatedly every morning. And taking full advantage of your 24 hours. Being a better father, mother, husband, wife, employee, entrepreneur, and boss. When we constantly work on ourselves and live that DRIVEN mindset, we improve everything and everyone around us. The impact starts every morning once you make that commitment to get up and get after it and focus on a DRIVEN mindset.

When we think about Jesus' sacrifice for us through his life. He was executed, which allows us to execute daily at free will. Execution at a high level takes maximum sacrifice. Execute your readiness plan and be intentional with the decision you are making that will cut down on distraction. Visualize your success for continued motivation. You will always be excited to execute.

NO EXCUSES, NEVER QUIT

The *N* in the DRIVEN mindset reminds me of my father's last days when he was fighting stomach cancer. It was the toughest time in my life to see the man I looked up to as a role model go through a disease that was relentless in slowing him down, which it did.

It slowed him down, but he fought hard to clean up his lifestyle choices. He fought to deal with the fact that chemotherapy was a horrible experience. He had a coming-to-Christ moment by professing that Jesus is the Lord. Despite all the hardships he was dealing with, he never quit or used an excuse for anything. He always kept a positive mindset so we would stay strong for him and continue living our lives to the fullest. My dad pulled me aside as he told me his last wishes if he went to his Lord. The part of his resignation to me, which has stuck with me till this day, was when he said, "Don't feel sorry for me; I lived a good life. Never stop living yours." When life gets hard, life does not stop. Neither should you. He wanted to continue to make an impact on the world one day at a time and one person at a time. He lived his life fully so that his kids could be set up for success. No excuse; just execute. In life, there will always be trials and tragedies that are totally out of our control. We will be mentally, spiritually, and physically tested.

Something can always be done as long as you have breath in your lungs and you are breathing under your own will. One of my dad's favorite sayings was, "When you have the will, you will find a way." Regardless of the situation, if you want something bad enough, you find a way to achieve it. That no-excuse mindset. That never-quit mentality is exactly what the *N* in DRIVEN means. Even though my dad did not win the battle with cancer in his body, his legacy lives through me. To impact many lives, get up every day and get after it like your life depends on it. We don't know when our last day is coming, so not a single day should be wasted.

Execute with small tasks first. Make sure you are setting yourself up for success with small, achievable goals day after day. You don't have to work out for an hour every day. You don't have to read 50 pages every day. You don't have to make 20 cold calls every day. But you have to start somewhere. Start small. Work out for 20 minutes a day. Read for 20 minutes a day. Make 5 cold calls a day. Small, sustainable activities help build confidence, consistency, and a sense of accomplishment. You are now bought in that this will be done. You get in a groove that you begin adding more time to the task. Crossing off a completed task gives you a high euphoria of success. You will begin to strive for more of this.

We often hear and say there are not enough hours in a day. That is an excuse. "I had something come up." That is an excuse. "I was too tired." That is another excuse. We even use the excuse, "I don't think I would even be better or more successful than I am now," or "Nothing has to change; I'm content with my life as it is." We give ourselves plenty of excuses to try and justify our actions to think it will help us feel better about not sticking to our desired goals. It is momentarily helping us because it is easy to have an excuse. That excuse begins to have power over our actions. We now don't allow ourselves to stay accountable to our dreams and desires. We need to stop doing what is easy. The easy roads often lead to no results. Taking the hard road, cutting off the excuse mindset, and getting a DRIVEN mindset with no excuses will lead you down the road to success. Excuses allow us to quit when times get rough. Excuses allow us to think our dreams and desires will never come true.

Speaking as a fitness professional, through all the years of my training, people strive to get to a place where they are content with their bodies. I can tell you this: 90% always strive for more. People start by saying one thing but then want more. "I want a flat stomach" turns into "I want a 6 pack." "I want to deadlift 315" turns into "I want to deadlift 405." When we accomplish a goal that we have set, we never become content. I made it this far; why not push and see what else I can accomplish?" It can have the same effect in everyday life. Start compounding small wins that are measurable and achievable. Acknowledge the sense of accomplishment. No excuses will allow you to never quit.

In a life where there are more obstacles and distractions in the way, we let the difficulties break us and hold us down. Sometimes, we give up way too easily because the end goal seems out of reach. Don't let your own self-mindset deter you from staying on the DRIVEN path. Our mindset is either our toughest competitor or our biggest cheerleader. If we allow ourselves to win those small minute battles with our own thoughts whenever they arise, we will compound so many important wins that will accelerate what we desire to achieve. An alarm must sound off in our brains when these excuses start to arise. It is likely that they have already wasted valuable time by taking you off course. We must regain focus and remember the acronym DRIVEN.

Quickly talk yourself through the *whys* of your Desire. Quickly look over your Readiness plan. Start saying those Intentional positive thoughts repeatedly in your head again. Allow that Vision to be completely clear once again. That will always Excite you once again to Execute. This constant mental action will be your solution to Never quit. That is the blueprint of winning every battle with your own self to align your focus on what you want to achieve. It will consistently prompt you to get up and get after it. I can actually say it is exactly what got me to write the book. I haven't written anything this long in my entire life. Reading and writing were not a part of my life before GOD spoke to me about keeping a DRIVEN mindset. I felt it would be a disservice to keep it to myself, especially when it can influence and make an impact on someone's life.

Set a goal, and then set your mind to achieve it. Remember to keep a DRIVEN mindset. Stay consistent and dedicated. When you think of DRIVEN, think of the dreams and the process of achieving them. Begin the work. Stay DRIVEN. You will become better each day, gradually of course. You will reach new heights. YOU will achieve what you Desire. You are DRIVEN. Always be gracious and thankful that God has blessed you with the ability to do so. Don't take it for granted because you might be unable to continue one day. GIVE HONOR AND glory to God all the time, for GOD loves you and wants you to live life to the fullest.

ABOUT THE AUTHOR

My passion is helping people reach their true potential. Whether it be physical, mental, spiritual. I have worked in the health & fitness professional field for 20 years transforming people into the best version of theirself. Working with thousands of people over my career I've learned what truly determines one's success.

Made in the USA
Middletown, DE
05 February 2024